ECO-ANXIETY GUIDE

COPING WITH CLIMATE CHANGE, STRESS AND FINDING HOPE

ANN E. SPRINGFIELD

Table of Contents

Introduction

Eco-Anxiety

Eco-anxiety is the term used to describe the worry, fear, or overwhelming feelings people have about climate change and the future of our planet. It's not just a casual worry—it's the kind of anxiety that can keep you awake at night, leave you feeling powerless, or make you constantly stressed about the state of the world.

Think of it like this: every time we hear about rising temperatures, endangered species, or severe weather events, it can create a feeling of helplessness. Eco-anxiety is the emotional response to these global challenges that are often out of our direct control. It's our mind's way of reacting to a situation that feels threatening, uncertain, and immense.

You are not alone if you've felt this way. People across the world are experiencing eco-anxiety, and it's a natural reaction to the alarming changes we see in our environment. Knowing that your worries are shared by many others can be comforting—it's a sign that you care deeply about our world.

The Global Picture: How Climate Change is Affecting Us Emotionally

Climate change isn't just impacting the planet physically; it's also affecting our mental and emotional health. Every time we see news reports about wildfires, floods, or melting ice caps, it's easy to feel overwhelmed, anxious, or even guilty. This sense of dread is especially common among young people, who are increasingly worried about the kind of world they will inherit.

For many, the emotional effects go beyond just feeling sad. It can feel like a constant weight on your shoulders, knowing that the environment is in peril and feeling unsure if there's anything you can do to help. In some communities already facing severe climate challenges, such as rising sea levels or drought, eco-anxiety becomes even more intense, as people witness the immediate impact on their homes and families.

It's important to acknowledge that these emotions are real and valid. They are a sign that we are aware and deeply connected to our surroundings. But they can also be draining, leading to feelings of hopelessness if we don't find ways to manage them effectively.

Why It's Okay to Feel Overwhelmed

Feeling overwhelmed by climate change is completely normal. We are constantly bombarded with information about environmental destruction, and the enormity of the challenge can make anyone feel small. It's okay to admit that the state of the world feels heavy, and that sometimes, it seems like too much to handle.

It's crucial to remember that eco-anxiety stems from a place of care. It means that you recognise the value of our planet, and you want a healthy future for yourself, your family, and all living beings. Acknowledging these emotions rather than ignoring them is the first step toward finding effective ways to cope. By understanding eco-anxiety, we can start turning our feelings into positive actions—big or small—that make a difference.

There is strength in our concern, and there is hope in our actions. By learning more about what we're experiencing, we can start to find ways to not only cope but also thrive while working towards a better future. Together, we can move from fear to hope, from overwhelm to empowerment.

Chapter 1: The Emotional Impact of Climate Change

The Science of Anxiety and Climate Change

Anxiety is a natural human response to situations that feel threatening or uncertain. Climate change, with all its unpredictable and potentially harmful impacts, is a major source of anxiety for many people around the world. But why is this?

Our brains are wired to react to threats—this is called the "fight or flight" response. When faced with a threat, our body releases stress hormones like adrenaline and cortisol, which prepare us to take action. In the past, this was useful for avoiding predators or other immediate dangers. Today, these same mechanisms kick in when we perceive a threat like climate change. The problem is that unlike a physical danger, climate change is vast, ongoing, and largely out of our individual control. This makes it challenging for our brains to find a clear solution, often leaving us feeling anxious and powerless.

Furthermore, the constant news cycle and social media updates about environmental disasters can make the issue seem even more inescapable. This "always-on" exposure feeds our anxiety because it keeps us in a heightened state of awareness, without any break to process or cope.

Recognising the Signs: How Eco-Anxiety Manifests

Eco-anxiety can manifest in many ways, both physically and emotionally. For some, it may be an ever-present worry in the back of their mind—a nagging fear that doesn't go away. For others, it might cause a more intense feeling of dread or panic whenever the topic of climate change comes up. Some common signs include:

- Restlessness and Trouble Sleeping: Many people find themselves lying awake at night, worrying about the future of the planet. The uncertainty of what might happen often makes it hard to switch off and rest.

- Feeling Overwhelmed or Helpless: When faced with the scale of climate change, it's easy to feel like any action we take is just a drop in the ocean. This sense of helplessness can lead to emotional exhaustion.

- Guilt and Shame: There's often a sense of personal responsibility that comes with eco-anxiety. People may feel guilty for driving a car, using plastic, or not doing enough to combat climate change. These feelings of guilt can add to the stress and anxiety, making us feel like we're part of the problem rather than part of the solution.

- Anger and Frustration: For many, eco-anxiety can also turn into anger—anger at governments for not doing enough, at corporations for their impact on the environment, or at others who seem indifferent. This anger is rooted in a desire for change but can be exhausting to carry day after day.

- Avoidance: Some people cope with eco-anxiety by trying to ignore it. They avoid news about climate change or even deny that it's happening to shield themselves from anxiety. This is a defence mechanism, a way for the mind to protect itself from feeling overwhelmed, but it can prevent people from engaging in positive actions.

Recognising these signs in yourself is an important first step. Understanding that your reactions are natural responses to a very real challenge can help reduce the self-judgement that often comes with eco-anxiety.

Stories from the Frontlines: Real People's Experiences

Sometimes, it helps to know that you are not alone—that others are also feeling what you feel. Let's take a look at some real people who have experienced eco-anxiety and how it has impacted their lives.

Emma's Story – The Mother Who Worries for Her Children

Emma is a mother of two young children. She describes feeling a deep sense of fear whenever she thinks about their future. "I want my kids to grow up in a world where they can breathe clean air, drink clean water, and see the beauty of nature," she says. "But every time I read about another environmental crisis, I feel like that future is slipping away." Emma's anxiety often leaves her feeling paralysed—she wants to help, but she doesn't know where to start, and this makes her feel like she's failing her children.

David's Story – The Activist Who Feels Burnt Out

David is a climate activist who has been involved in protests, campaigns, and community initiatives for years. While he feels proud of the work he's done, the slow pace of change has taken a toll on him. "There are days when it feels like no matter what we do, nothing is enough," David admits. "I've been to rallies, written to politicians, and worked tirelessly, but sometimes, I feel like we're not making a difference." David's story highlights the emotional exhaustion that can come from feeling like you're fighting a battle that's too big to win.

Sophia's Story – The Teenager Who Feels Overwhelmed

Sophia, a high school student, began feeling anxious about climate change when she learned about it in school. "It's scary to think that by the time I'm an adult, the world might be a much harsher place to live in," she says. She often finds herself worrying about the things she can't control—rising sea levels, wildfires, species going extinct. It makes her feel small and powerless, and sometimes, it's hard for her to enjoy everyday life without thinking about the bigger picture.

These stories show that eco-anxiety can affect people of all ages and backgrounds, and it can be triggered by a variety of experiences. Emma, David, and Sophia all feel overwhelmed, but they also care deeply about the planet, which is why they feel this way. Their stories remind us that eco-anxiety is a natural response to the situation we're in, and that there is strength in acknowledging these feelings. By understanding that others share our fears and frustrations, we can find ways to support each other and move forward together.

Chapter 2: Building Resilience – Emotional Coping Strategies

Acceptance as a First Step

One of the hardest but most important steps in dealing with eco-anxiety is acceptance. This doesn't mean giving up or ignoring the problem—it means acknowledging that climate change is real, it is here, and it's okay to feel overwhelmed by it. Acceptance allows us to recognise that we are facing a big challenge without letting fear control us.

Imagine being caught in a sudden rainstorm. If you try to ignore it or pretend it's not happening, you end up feeling miserable, wet, and frustrated. But if you accept that it's raining and either find shelter or embrace the rain, you're better able to adapt. The same goes for eco-anxiety. When we accept our feelings, we allow ourselves to process them instead of trying to fight against them.

Acceptance is powerful because it frees up the energy we spend on denial or fear. It's okay to admit that we don't have all the answers or that we're scared. By accepting the reality of climate change and our emotions about it, we can start focusing on what we can do—both for the planet and for our own well-being.

Mindfulness and Living in the Present

Mindfulness is a tool that helps us focus on the present moment rather than getting lost in worries about the future. Eco-anxiety often comes from thinking too far ahead—wondering what the world will look like in 10, 20, or 50 years. These thoughts can be overwhelming, making it difficult to enjoy the here and now.

Mindfulness encourages us to slow down and pay attention to what is happening right now. It can be as simple as taking a deep breath, feeling the ground beneath your feet, or noticing the warmth of the sun on your skin. These small actions help bring you back to the present, reminding you that while the future is uncertain, there is still beauty and calm to be found in the moment.

One simple exercise you can do is called "5-4-3-2-1." When you start feeling anxious, pause and identify:

- 5 things you can see (a tree outside, your coffee mug, etc.)
- 4 things you can touch (your shirt, a table, etc.)
- 3 things you can hear (birds chirping, the hum of a fan, etc.)
- 2 things you can smell (the scent of flowers, food cooking, etc.)
- 1 thing you can taste (a sip of water, gum, etc.)

This exercise helps you stay grounded and brings your attention back to what's real and tangible around you. Mindfulness isn't about ignoring the big problems—it's about giving your mind a break from the constant stress of thinking about the future and finding peace in the present.

Emotional Self-Care: A Daily Practice to Stay Grounded

Taking care of your emotional health is just as important as caring for your physical health. When dealing with eco-anxiety, practising emotional self-care can help you stay grounded, calm, and capable of taking positive action.

1. Limit Your News Intake

Staying informed is important, but constant exposure to negative news can make eco-anxiety worse. It's okay to take breaks from the news, especially if you feel it's affecting your mood. You could set a specific time each day to catch up on the latest updates and then move on to something positive. Remember, taking care of yourself doesn't mean ignoring the world—it means finding balance.

2. Connect with Supportive People

Talking to others who share your concerns can be incredibly comforting. Find friends, family members, or support groups who understand what you're going through. Just knowing you're not alone can help lighten the load. Sharing your worries with someone who listens and cares can bring a sense of relief, and sometimes, you might even find new ideas or solutions together.

3. Find Joy in Everyday Activities

Eco-anxiety can sometimes make us feel guilty for experiencing joy, but finding happiness is essential for staying strong. Whether it's gardening, cooking, playing a musical instrument, or simply watching your favourite show, doing things that bring you happiness is important. Joy doesn't mean you've forgotten about the challenges we face; it means you're building the strength to face them.

4. Practice Gratitude

Gratitude is a simple yet powerful practice. Every day, take a moment to think about something you are thankful for. It could be the fresh air you're breathing, the laughter you shared with a friend, or the beauty of a flower in your garden. Gratitude helps shift your focus from the things that are out of your control to the positive aspects of your life. It's a reminder that while the world has its problems, it also has its wonders.

5. Create a Routine

Having a daily routine can help you feel more in control. It doesn't have to be complex—just having set times for meals, exercise, or relaxation can make a big difference in managing anxiety. Including some time for reflection or relaxation—like journaling or meditating—can help you process your thoughts and emotions effectively.

Building resilience is about taking small steps every day to care for yourself and nurture your emotional strength. It's about finding ways to cope with the anxiety, not by ignoring it, but by recognising that there are moments of peace, joy, and hope even in a challenging situation. By practising acceptance, mindfulness, and emotional self-care, you can stay grounded and grow stronger in the face of eco-anxiety.

Chapter 3: Finding Hope in a Changing World

Positive Action as an Antidote to Anxiety

One of the most effective ways to cope with eco-anxiety is by taking action. When we feel overwhelmed by the scale of climate change, it's easy to feel powerless. But doing something—no matter how small—can make a big difference, not just for the environment but for our mental health as well. Positive action is like medicine for anxiety. It shifts our focus from fear to purpose, replacing feelings of helplessness with empowerment.

You don't need to do everything perfectly to make a difference. It could be as simple as reducing your plastic use, planting a tree, joining a local clean-up, or even talking to friends and family about the environment. Every positive action we take is a step towards a better future, and each step adds up.

Think of action as a light in the dark. When you're in a dark room, even a small candle can make a big difference. In the same way, every effort you make brightens the world just a little bit more. Taking action not only helps the planet but also provides you with a sense of purpose and control. Instead of focusing on what you can't change, you start to see what you can do, and that brings hope.

Celebrating Progress: Environmental Wins Around the World

It's easy to get caught up in the negative news, but it's important to remember that there have been many environmental successes too. These positive changes remind us that progress is possible and that our efforts are not in vain. When we celebrate these wins, we nurture hope and motivation, showing that change can happen when people come together.

Here are just a few examples of environmental wins that deserve celebration:

1. The Ozone Layer Recovery

Years ago, scientists discovered that chemicals like CFCs were damaging the ozone layer—a protective shield that guards Earth from harmful ultraviolet rays. Thanks to international cooperation, countries came together to ban these harmful substances, and now, the ozone layer is slowly healing. This shows that when the world acts together, even large-scale problems can be fixed.

2. Wildlife Conservation Success Stories

Several species that were once on the brink of extinction have made a comeback thanks to conservation efforts. Animals like the humpback whale, giant panda, and bald eagle have seen significant recovery because people took action to protect them. These stories remind us that nature is resilient and can recover when given the chance.

3. Growth of Renewable Energy

Renewable energy sources like wind and solar power are expanding rapidly around the world. More countries are investing in clean energy, reducing their reliance on fossil fuels. This shift is helping reduce carbon emissions and shows that a future powered by sustainable energy is possible.

4. Plastic Bans

Countries and cities around the world are taking a stand against plastic pollution by banning single-use plastics. This change is helping reduce the amount of plastic waste that ends up in our oceans and rivers. It's proof that policy changes, driven by public demand, can make a real difference.

These wins may not solve every problem, but they show that progress is possible. By focusing on these positive changes, we can remind ourselves that our actions have an impact, and that we are not alone in this journey. There are millions of people working for a better planet, and together, we are making a difference.

The Power of Community and Collective Action

While individual actions are important, collective action is where real, lasting change often happens. There's something incredibly powerful about people coming together for a shared cause. Community and collective action not only amplify the impact of our efforts but also help us feel connected and supported.

1. Strength in Numbers
When you join a group—whether it's a local environmental organisation, an online community, or a neighbourhood clean-up—you're not only contributing to the cause but also gaining support

from others who understand what you're feeling. Eco-anxiety often makes us feel alone, but being part of a community shows us that we are not alone. It's easier to face challenges when you're surrounded by people who share your passion and determination.

2. Turning Anxiety into Action
Communities have a unique ability to channel collective anxiety into meaningful action. Protests, petitions, clean-up drives, and educational events are often more effective when organised by a group rather than by individuals. There's power in numbers, and that power can lead to real change. Remember, many of the biggest changes in history started with small groups of dedicated people who believed in a better future.

3. Supporting Each Other
Community is also about emotional support. Sometimes, it's just as important to have someone to talk to about your concerns as it is to take action.

By connecting with others, you can share your fears, hopes, and ideas. It's comforting to know that you're part of something bigger, and it helps turn what might feel like an overwhelming burden into a shared mission.

4. Learning and Growing Together
Communities are a great source of knowledge. You can learn practical skills, hear about successful projects, and discover new ways to make a difference. Whether you're learning how to start a compost pile, use less water, or contact your local government about environmental policies, being part of a group helps you gain the confidence and skills you need to take action.

Examples of Collective Success

There are numerous examples of collective action making a real difference. In many places, grassroots movements have successfully pressured governments to pass laws that protect the environment. School strikes for climate, led by young people around the world, have brought attention to the urgency of climate action. These movements show that when people work together, they can demand and create change on a larger scale.

Finding hope in a changing world isn't always easy, but it's possible. By taking positive action, celebrating the progress we've already made, and joining forces with others, we can move from a place of fear to one of hope and empowerment. Remember, even though the challenges we face are big, we are not alone—and together, we can make a difference.

Chapter 4: Climate Advocacy and Your Role

Becoming an Advocate: Finding Your Voice

Climate advocacy is about standing up for the planet, using your voice to call for change, and encouraging others to do the same. But becoming an advocate doesn't mean you have to be an expert or dedicate your life to activism. It's about finding a way to make your voice heard that feels right for you.

Advocacy can start with something as simple as talking to friends and family about why climate change matters. Many people care about the environment but may not understand the urgency. By sharing what you know, you can help others see why it's important to act now.

Finding your voice means figuring out what you're passionate about and how you can contribute. Maybe you enjoy writing—consider writing letters to your local government officials, asking them to take stronger action. If you're comfortable with public speaking, you could talk at community events or participate in climate rallies. The key is to use your strengths in a way that makes an impact. Remember, every voice matters, and sometimes it only takes one person to inspire many others to get involved.

How to Engage with Local, National, and International Climate Movements

Once you feel ready to take the next step, getting involved with organised climate movements can amplify your efforts. There are movements at every level—local, national, and international—and each one has its own way of making a difference. Engaging with these movements allows you to be part of something bigger and see the impact of collective action.

1. Local Movements

Starting locally can be one of the most effective ways to create change. Your town or city is where you live, and changes there can directly improve your life and the environment around you. Look for community clean-up events, tree-planting initiatives, or workshops on sustainability. You can also connect with local environmental groups to learn about ongoing projects or even start one yourself, like a community garden. Engaging with local governments—attending city council meetings or writing to representatives—can also push for changes like improving recycling programs or creating more green spaces.

2. National Movements

National climate movements often aim to influence laws and policies. Supporting these movements can mean signing petitions, attending rallies, or

contacting national leaders to demand climate
action. Many national organisations have online
resources to help you get involved, such as guides
for contacting your representatives or tips for
organising events. Being part of a national
movement helps amplify your voice and sends a
stronger message to those in power: that people
across the country want change.

3. International Movements
Climate change is a global issue, and international
movements work to bring countries together to find
solutions. While it may seem like something beyond
our individual control, joining international efforts
can still make a difference. Many organisations
operate worldwide and provide ways for people to
contribute, from social media campaigns to
international petitions. You can also follow and
support global events like Earth Hour or participate
in climate strikes that take place in cities around
the world. These actions help show world leaders

that people everywhere are watching and care about the planet.

Making a Difference: Everyday Changes That Matter

Advocacy isn't just about rallies and petitions—it's also about how you live your life every day. Our daily choices can add up to make a big difference for the environment, and they can set an example for others to follow.

1. Reduce, Reuse, Recycle

It's an old saying, but it's still one of the most powerful ways to reduce waste. Start by reducing what you use—buying fewer things and avoiding single-use items. Reusing items, like using a reusable bag or water bottle, helps cut down on waste. Recycling what can't be reused means that fewer materials end up in landfills. These small actions add up and help reduce the strain on our planet.

2. Eat with the Planet in Mind

The food we eat has an impact on the environment, especially when it comes to meat production, which contributes significantly to greenhouse gases. You don't have to give up meat entirely if that doesn't work for you, but even reducing how much you eat can make a difference. Try adding more plant-based meals to your diet, buying locally grown produce, or supporting sustainable food brands. It's about making choices that are better for both your health and the planet.

3. Use Less Energy

Reducing your energy use at home is another way to make a difference. Turn off lights when you leave a room, unplug devices when they're not in use, and consider using energy-efficient light bulbs or appliances. If possible, use renewable energy options, like solar panels. These changes can help lower greenhouse gas emissions and save you money on energy bills.

4. Travel Smart

Transportation is a major source of carbon emissions, but small changes can help reduce your impact. Consider walking or biking for short trips—it's not only better for the environment but also great for your health. Carpooling, using public transport, or driving a fuel-efficient vehicle are other good options. If you need to fly, look into carbon offset programs that help balance the emissions from your trip.

5. Support Eco-Friendly Companies

Where you spend your money matters. Supporting companies that prioritise sustainability can help drive change in the market. Look for businesses that use renewable materials, produce less waste, and treat their workers well. When you support these companies, you help show that there's a demand for sustainable products, encouraging others to follow suit.

In all, advocacy and everyday changes go hand-in-hand. You don't need to be an environmental scientist or an activist to make a difference. By finding your voice, getting involved in movements that align with your passions, and making environmentally conscious choices, you become part of the solution. The more people join in, the bigger the impact we can make.

Remember, the goal isn't to be perfect—it's to make progress. Every positive action counts, and when combined with the actions of others, it can create real, lasting change. Advocacy is about hope and believing that we have the power to make a difference, no matter how small our actions may seem.

Chapter 5: Lifestyle Changes to Mitigate Eco-Anxiety

Adopting Sustainable Practices at Home

One of the best ways to reduce eco-anxiety is by making changes right in your own home. Our home is where we feel most in control, and making it more sustainable helps create a space that reflects your values. Sustainable practices are not just good for the environment; they can also provide a sense of purpose, help save money, and make your living space healthier and more enjoyable.

Start by taking small steps, such as switching to energy-efficient light bulbs, reducing water usage, or using natural cleaning products instead of those filled with harsh chemicals. Each small change can have a positive impact on the environment, and knowing that you are doing your part helps reduce the feelings of helplessness that often come with eco-anxiety.

Consider starting a compost pile in your garden or even a small compost bin if you live in an apartment. Composting reduces food waste and creates nutrient-rich material that you can use to help plants grow. Seeing the tangible results of your efforts—turning kitchen scraps into soil—can be incredibly rewarding. It's a reminder that nature is resilient and that you are playing a part in helping it thrive.

Another sustainable practice is being mindful of electricity use. Turn off appliances when they're not in use, use power strips, and take advantage of natural light during the day. Not only does this reduce your carbon footprint, but it also creates a more peaceful atmosphere, free from the constant hum of machines.

The Role of Diet, Transportation, and Waste Reduction

Making sustainable choices in your diet, transportation, and waste habits can go a long way in reducing both your carbon footprint and your eco-anxiety. These lifestyle changes don't have to be drastic—small shifts can have a significant impact.

1. Diet

Our diet plays a major role in our environmental impact. One simple way to be more sustainable is to eat more plant-based meals. This doesn't mean you need to give up meat entirely, but reducing how often you eat it can help lower greenhouse gas emissions. Try incorporating "meatless Mondays" or focusing on more fruits, vegetables, legumes, and whole grains throughout the week. Eating with the environment in mind also means choosing locally grown food whenever possible. Not only does this support local farmers, but it also reduces the emissions involved in transporting food over long distances.

Being intentional about your diet can help ease eco-anxiety because it gives you a direct way to make a difference. You're contributing to a more sustainable world with every meal, and that sense of positive action can be empowering.

2. Transportation

Transportation is another area where small changes can make a big difference. Walking or biking for short trips is a great way to cut down on emissions while also staying active, which is good for both physical and mental health. If biking or walking isn't an option, consider carpooling, taking public transportation, or using a more fuel-efficient vehicle. Even planning your trips more efficiently—like combining errands into one outing—can help reduce emissions.

Transportation choices can often feel like a direct contribution to either the problem or the solution. When you choose a sustainable way to travel, it feels good to know that you are actively making a decision that benefits the planet. This sense of control is a powerful way to ease eco-anxiety.

3. Waste Reduction

Reducing waste is another meaningful way to live more sustainably. It starts with being mindful of what you buy. Opt for products with minimal packaging, use reusable bags, and avoid single-use items whenever possible. Recycling is important, but reducing and reusing are even better because they prevent waste from being created in the first place.

Think about how much plastic we use daily—from water bottles to shopping bags—and consider how you can cut back. Replacing single-use plastic items with reusable alternatives not only helps the environment but also gives you a sense of purpose.

You're making choices that align with your values, and this can help alleviate eco-anxiety. Seeing less waste in your own home can make a big difference in how you feel about the larger issue.

Minimalism and How It Can Reduce Stress and Anxiety

Minimalism is about simplifying your life—focusing on what truly matters and letting go of the excess. It's a lifestyle that helps reduce stress, saves money, and, importantly, is beneficial for the planet. Embracing minimalism can be a powerful way to cope with eco-anxiety because it encourages us to shift our focus away from consuming and accumulating towards appreciating and conserving.

Many of us are overwhelmed by the sheer amount of "stuff" we own. Clutter can contribute to feelings of anxiety, and often, the things we buy don't bring us the happiness we expect. Minimalism helps us break free from the cycle of consumerism by encouraging us to think carefully before making a purchase. When we buy less, we reduce the demand for production and transportation, which leads to fewer emissions and less resource depletion.

Minimalism isn't just about material items—it's also about simplifying our schedules and commitments. Reducing unnecessary activities allows more time to enjoy what really matters, like spending time with loved ones or connecting with nature. This simplification brings a sense of calm, and it also allows us to be more mindful of how our actions affect the world around us.

Imagine having fewer things to clean, organise, or worry about. A minimalist approach to life creates more physical space and mental space, allowing you to focus on what's important and let go of what's not. This helps reduce anxiety, including eco-anxiety, by eliminating some of the excess noise that often contributes to stress.

Minimalism also naturally leads to a more sustainable lifestyle. When we stop buying things we don't need, we reduce waste, consume fewer resources, and focus more on experiences rather than possessions. This shift can bring a deeper sense of fulfillment—one that's not tied to owning things but rather to living intentionally and in harmony with the environment.

To conclude, making sustainable lifestyle changes is one of the best ways to address eco-anxiety. By adopting sustainable practices at home, making conscious choices about diet, transportation, and waste, and embracing minimalism, you are not only helping the planet but also taking meaningful steps to take care of your mental well-being.

These changes don't have to happen overnight, and you don't need to do everything perfectly. Start with small steps and build from there. Each choice you make, no matter how small, contributes to a healthier planet and a more hopeful future. And as you make these changes, you'll find that your feelings of anxiety start to lessen, replaced by a sense of purpose and connection to the world around you.

Chapter 6: Building Community Support Networks

The Importance of Community in Times of Crisis

In times of crisis, there's nothing quite like the comfort and strength that comes from being part of a community. When we face big challenges, like climate change, the emotional load can feel too heavy to carry alone. But when we share that burden with others, it becomes a lot more manageable. Being part of a supportive community gives us a sense of belonging and reminds us that we are not alone in our worries.

Community is crucial because it provides emotional support. Just talking to someone who understands

what you're going through can be a huge relief.
Eco-anxiety can feel isolating, but knowing that
others share your concerns makes it easier to cope.
When people come together, they can share ideas,
support each other emotionally, and work together
to create positive change.

Communities are also powerful in taking action.
When a group of people shares a common goal, they
can make a bigger impact than any one person
could alone. Whether it's organising a local
clean-up, planting trees, or advocating for
environmental changes, communities amplify the
power of individuals. Working together not only
makes a bigger difference for the planet but also
helps ease anxiety by turning feelings of
helplessness into collective action.

How to Form Eco-Anxiety Support Groups

If you're feeling overwhelmed by eco-anxiety, chances are others in your community are too. Creating a support group is a great way to bring people together to share their experiences, learn from one another, and find strength in numbers. You don't need to be an expert or a leader to start a group—you just need to be someone who cares and wants to connect with others.

1. Finding People Who Share Your Concerns

Start by reaching out to friends, family, or neighbours who are also interested in environmental issues. You could post on social media or community boards, letting people know you're starting an eco-anxiety support group. Many people may feel the same way you do but haven't had the chance to talk about it yet, and they'll be grateful to have a space to share their thoughts.

2. Creating a Safe Space

The goal of a support group is to provide a safe, non-judgmental space where people can share their feelings. It's important that everyone in the group feels heard and respected. You can start by having open discussions where everyone gets a chance to talk, without fear of being judged or dismissed. Remember, eco-anxiety affects everyone differently, and each person's feelings are valid.

3. Meeting Regularly

Setting up regular meetings helps create a sense of continuity and support. These meetings could be in-person at a community centre, a local café, or even outdoors in a park. If meeting in person isn't possible, virtual meetings can work just as well. The important part is creating a routine that people can rely on—a time when they know they can come together, share, and find support.

4. Sharing Ideas and Solutions

In addition to sharing feelings, support groups can be a great way to share ideas and solutions. Members can talk about what they're doing to cope with eco-anxiety, such as mindfulness practices or sustainable lifestyle changes, and support each other in taking positive actions. When people work together, they can come up with creative solutions to local issues, which can help everyone feel more empowered.

5. Engaging in Group Activities

Doing activities as a group can also help members feel more connected and empowered. You could organise a tree-planting day, a neighbourhood clean-up, or a letter-writing campaign to local officials. These activities provide a sense of purpose and remind everyone that they are capable of making a difference.

Building Resilient, Eco-Friendly Communities

Communities are stronger when they work together, and building an eco-friendly community is about making changes that benefit everyone. A resilient community isn't just about being prepared for challenges—it's about creating a supportive environment where people can thrive, even in the face of difficulties like climate change.

1. Connecting with Your Neighbours

Building a resilient, eco-friendly community starts with getting to know the people around you. Take the time to connect with your neighbours, whether it's by starting conversations, organising a block party, or creating a neighbourhood group chat. These connections are the foundation of a strong community—people are more likely to help each other when they know each other well.

2. Sharing Resources

One way to make a community more sustainable is to share resources. This could mean creating a community garden where everyone contributes and benefits, starting a tool-sharing program so that not everyone needs to buy their own tools, or organising carpooling groups. By sharing, the community reduces waste, saves money, and strengthens bonds.

3. Supporting Local Initiatives

Supporting local businesses and initiatives is another great way to build an eco-friendly community. Local farmers' markets, repair cafés, and sustainable shops all contribute to the health of the community and the environment. By supporting these initiatives, you're helping keep money within the community and encouraging sustainable practices.

4. <u>Educating and Raising Awareness</u>
Education is a key part of building resilience.
Hosting workshops or informational events on
topics like composting, recycling, or growing your
own food can help community members learn new
skills and become more self-sufficient. These events
can also be a way to bring people together and
create a sense of shared purpose.

5. <u>Preparing for Climate Challenges Together</u>
Climate change can bring unexpected challenges,
like extreme weather or power outages. A resilient
community is one that's prepared for these
situations. Work with your community to create
emergency plans—know who might need extra help
in an emergency, and make sure everyone has the
resources they need. Being prepared reduces
anxiety and builds confidence, as people know they
have the support of their community during
difficult times.

Yes. Building a supportive community is one of the most powerful ways to cope with eco-anxiety. Whether it's creating a small support group, participating in community activities, or working to make your neighbourhood more sustainable, being part of a community provides emotional support, a sense of belonging, and a feeling of empowerment.

When people come together, they can share the weight of their worries, work together towards solutions, and find comfort in knowing they are not alone. By creating and participating in community support networks, you're not just helping yourself—you're helping others, building resilience, and contributing to a healthier, more connected world. Together, we are stronger, and together, we can make a difference.

Chapter 7: Connecting with Nature for Emotional Well-being

Ecotherapy and the Healing Power of Nature

Have you ever felt calmer after a walk in the woods, a visit to a park, or simply spending time surrounded by plants? There's a reason for that—being in nature has a powerful ability to heal and uplift us. This is what ecotherapy is all about: using nature as a way to improve our mental and emotional well-being.

Ecotherapy is a simple but effective way to reduce feelings of stress, anxiety, and even depression. It's based on the idea that humans are deeply connected to the natural world, and when we spend time in it, we naturally feel better. Unlike the hectic, noisy environments of cities or workplaces, nature provides a place of quiet and calm where we can slow down, breathe deeply, and let go of the worries that weigh us down.

Imagine sitting by a river, listening to the sound of the flowing water, or feeling the soft crunch of leaves under your feet in a forest. These experiences are not only peaceful but also grounding—they remind us that we are part of something larger, something timeless. Nature has a way of putting things into perspective. When we feel overwhelmed by the challenges of climate change or everyday stress, spending time outside can bring us back to the present and remind us of the beauty that still exists in the world.

Reconnecting Through Outdoor Activities and Green Spaces

Reconnecting with nature doesn't require a grand adventure into the wilderness—it can be as simple as spending more time outdoors, appreciating the natural world around you. Whether it's a walk in a nearby park, a hike on a local trail, or even gardening in your backyard, outdoor activities are a wonderful way to reconnect with nature and ease eco-anxiety.

1. Walking in Nature

One of the easiest ways to enjoy nature is to go for a walk. Find a nearby park or trail, or simply take a stroll through your neighbourhood. Walking in a natural setting helps you clear your mind, and the physical activity releases endorphins, which are natural mood boosters. It's not about speed or distance; it's about being present and appreciating the sights, sounds, and smells around you. Take a moment to notice the colours of the leaves, the chirping of birds, or the warmth of the sun on your skin. These small details help bring you back to the present moment, easing feelings of worry or stress.

2. Gardening

Gardening is a wonderful way to reconnect with the earth. Planting flowers, herbs, or vegetables lets you get your hands in the soil, feel connected to the cycle of growth, and create something beautiful or nourishing. Gardening is also a great way to witness resilience—watching a seedling grow into a healthy plant shows that, even in challenging conditions, life finds a way. This can be a powerful reminder of our own resilience, especially when we're feeling overwhelmed by the problems of the world.

3. Outdoor Hobbies

Taking up an outdoor hobby, like birdwatching, fishing, or photography, can also be a great way to spend more time in nature. These activities encourage you to slow down and observe the natural world, helping you develop a deeper appreciation for it. For example, birdwatching might help you notice how different birds behave, while photography can make you pay attention to the beauty in the smallest details—a flower, a leaf, or the way sunlight filters through the trees. These activities can bring a sense of joy and wonder, reminding us why protecting nature is worth it.

4. Visiting Green Spaces

If you live in a city, finding nature can feel challenging, but there are often more opportunities than you think. Visiting parks, botanical gardens, or even green rooftops can give you a much-needed break from urban noise. Spending time in these spaces, surrounded by trees and greenery, can be incredibly calming and restorative. Green spaces offer a place to sit quietly, enjoy the fresh air, and feel a sense of connection to the natural world, even if it's just for a short while.

Nature-Based Mindfulness Practices

Mindfulness is about being fully present in the moment, and when practiced in nature, it can be even more powerful. Nature-based mindfulness helps us slow down and truly connect with our surroundings, easing our anxiety and bringing a sense of peace. Here are a few simple nature-based mindfulness practices that you can try:

1. Grounding with Bare Feet

Grounding, or "earthing," involves connecting physically with the earth by walking barefoot on grass, soil, or sand. This simple act can help you feel grounded and connected to the natural world. Take a few minutes to stand barefoot in a park or garden, and feel the texture of the earth beneath you. Close your eyes and take a few deep breaths. This practice can be very calming and can help you feel more rooted and stable, especially when you're feeling anxious.

2. Breathing with Nature

Another mindfulness practice is to sit quietly in nature and focus on your breath. Find a comfortable spot—under a tree, by a river, or in a garden. Close your eyes and take slow, deep breaths. As you breathe in, imagine that you're breathing in the calmness of nature. As you breathe out, imagine letting go of your worries and stress. Let the natural sounds around you—like the rustling of leaves or the songs of birds—guide your breath and bring a sense of calm.

3. Nature Observation

Take a few minutes to observe something in nature closely. It could be a flower, a tree, or even a small insect. Notice the colours, the shapes, the movements. By focusing all your attention on this one natural object, you allow your mind to rest from the constant worry about the past or future. This simple practice helps you connect with the present and appreciate the small wonders of the natural world.

4. Listening to Nature

Another way to practice mindfulness is by listening. Sit or lie down in a natural setting, close your eyes, and focus on the sounds around you. Maybe it's the wind rustling through the trees, birds singing, or the distant sound of water. Listening deeply helps us feel connected to the world around us and brings a sense of peace and stillness that is often missing from our daily lives.

In conclusion, nature has an incredible ability to heal and uplift us. Whether it's through ecotherapy, outdoor activities, or mindfulness practices, connecting with nature can provide a much-needed break from the stress and anxiety of everyday life, including eco-anxiety. The natural world reminds us that there is beauty, resilience, and hope all around us—even in the face of challenges.

The next time you feel overwhelmed, take a moment to step outside, breathe in the fresh air, and reconnect with the natural world. Whether it's a walk in the park, a gardening session, or a quiet moment listening to the wind, these simple acts can bring you back to a place of calm and help you remember why our connection to the earth is so precious. When we care for nature, we care for ourselves, and in doing so, we find hope, strength, and the resilience to keep moving forward.

Chapter 8: Talking About Eco-Anxiety with Loved Ones

How to Have Open Conversations About Climate Change

Talking about climate change, especially with those we care about, can be challenging. It's a topic that can bring up strong emotions—fear, frustration, even anger—and it's easy to feel misunderstood or alone in your concerns. However, having open and honest conversations with loved ones is an important step in coping with eco-anxiety and helping others understand why this issue matters so much.

1. Start by Sharing Your Feelings.

A good way to begin the conversation is by talking about your own feelings. You might say, "I've been feeling really worried about what's happening with the environment lately," or "I've noticed that I'm feeling anxious about climate change." This helps others understand that the topic is personally meaningful to you, and it makes the conversation more about sharing than convincing. Talking about how you feel, rather than just the facts, makes it easier for others to relate and respond with empathy.

2. Listen Without Judgement.

Not everyone is going to feel the same way you do about climate change, and that's okay. When discussing eco-anxiety, it's important to listen to what others have to say without being judgmental or dismissive. Some people might not know much about the topic, while others might feel overwhelmed by it. The goal is to create a space where everyone feels comfortable sharing their thoughts and feelings. By listening, you show that you care about their perspective, which can help build understanding and trust.

3. Focus on Hope and Solutions.

Conversations about climate change can quickly turn gloomy, which can leave everyone feeling more anxious. Instead, try to focus on hope and positive actions. Talk about the steps people are taking to make a difference, both big and small. For example, you could mention a local clean-up project, an inspiring environmental leader, or even the sustainable choices you're making in your daily life. By focusing on solutions, you help keep the conversation productive and uplifting, rather than adding to feelings of helplessness.

4. Know When to Step Back.

Not every conversation will go as planned, and that's okay. If you sense that someone isn't receptive or the discussion is becoming too tense, it's fine to step back and revisit it later. Remember that change takes time, and planting a seed now may lead to a more open conversation in the future.

Supporting Others While Managing Your Own Stress

When it comes to climate change, you might find yourself being the one that others turn to for support, especially if they know you're passionate about the environment. While it's great to be a source of support, it's important to take care of your own mental health as well. If you're already struggling with eco-anxiety, trying to help others can sometimes add to your stress, so finding a balance is key.

1. Set Boundaries

It's okay to set boundaries when talking about climate change. You don't always have to be the one to answer questions or provide emotional support, especially if you're feeling overwhelmed. You can let others know that while you care about the issue, you need to take a break sometimes for your own well-being. For example, you might say, "I'd love to talk more about this, but I need to take some time for myself right now." Setting boundaries doesn't mean you don't care—it means you're taking care of yourself so that you can continue to be supportive in the long run.

2. Share Resources

Instead of always being the one to provide answers, consider sharing resources that have helped you. This could be a book, an article, or a documentary that explains climate issues in a way that's easy to understand. By pointing others toward helpful resources, you can support them without feeling like you have to carry the entire emotional load yourself.

3. Practice Self-Care

Supporting others can be emotionally draining, especially when it comes to something as big and complex as climate change. Make sure to prioritise your own self-care—whether that's taking time for a walk, meditating, enjoying a hobby, or simply unplugging from the news for a while. The better you care for yourself, the more energy and resilience you'll have to support those around you.

4. Remember You're Not Alone

It's easy to feel like the weight of the world is on your shoulders, but remember that you are not alone in caring for the planet. There are millions of people out there working toward the same goal. Reach out to support groups, friends, or communities who share your concerns. Connecting with others who understand what you're feeling can help lighten the load and remind you that you're part of a larger movement.

Raising Climate-Conscious Kids Without Instilling Fear

If you're a parent or work with children, you might be wondering how to talk to them about climate change without causing unnecessary fear or anxiety. It's important to raise climate-conscious kids who care about the planet, but it's equally important to do so in a way that is age-appropriate and hopeful.

1. Keep It Simple and Honest.

When talking to kids about climate change, it's best to keep the information simple and honest. Children don't need to know all the scary details, but they do benefit from understanding that the environment is important and that we need to take care of it. You could explain that pollution is bad for animals and plants, but that we can help by recycling, saving water, and planting trees. Keeping the message clear and focusing on solutions helps kids feel like they can make a difference.

2. Focus on Empowerment.

Instead of focusing on the negative aspects of climate change, talk about the positive actions they can take. Kids love feeling like they are helping, so give them opportunities to get involved. You could start a small garden together, pick up litter at the park, or learn about endangered animals and how to protect them. These activities not only teach kids about caring for the environment but also give them a sense of empowerment, which helps counter feelings of fear.

3. Make It Fun.

Kids learn best when they're having fun, so try to make environmental education enjoyable. You could read books about nature, watch educational videos, or go on nature walks to explore the local environment. Encouraging curiosity helps children develop a love for nature, which naturally leads to wanting to protect it. By making it fun, you're teaching them that caring for the planet isn't just important—it's also rewarding.

4. Be a Role Model.

Children learn a lot by watching the adults around them. By making environmentally friendly choices in your daily life—such as using reusable bags, conserving energy, or biking instead of driving—you're setting an example for them to follow. When kids see you caring for the planet, they learn that these actions are normal and important.

5. Reassure Them.

It's natural for children to have questions and worries about the world. When these questions come up, it's important to reassure them. Let them know that there are many people, including scientists, communities, and leaders, working hard to protect the planet. Emphasise that even though climate change is a big problem, there are many people making a difference, and every little action counts.

Talking about eco-anxiety with loved ones can be challenging, but it's also an important way to build understanding, support one another, and inspire positive action. By approaching these conversations with empathy, openness, and a focus on hope, you can help those around you understand why the environment matters to you—and why it should matter to them too.

Supporting others while managing your own stress is all about finding balance and knowing that it's okay to take breaks. And when it comes to raising children, the goal is to nurture their love for the planet in a way that empowers them, rather than instilling fear. By sharing your concerns, listening

to others, and focusing on hope and positive
actions, you can help create a supportive
environment where everyone feels encouraged to
care for our world.

Chapter 9: The Role of Governments and Corporations

How Policy Changes Can Alleviate Eco-Anxiety

Governments play a huge role in addressing climate change. They have the power to make decisions that affect entire countries—setting rules, providing funding for green initiatives, and leading by example. When governments take strong action to fight climate change, it helps people feel more hopeful about the future and can significantly reduce eco-anxiety.

One of the reasons eco-anxiety can feel overwhelming is the sense that our individual actions aren't enough to fix such a big problem.

This is where government policies can make a real difference. Policies like reducing carbon emissions, investing in renewable energy, and setting up conservation areas show that leaders are taking the problem seriously. When we see our governments taking meaningful action, it reminds us that we're not in this fight alone—there are people in positions of power who are working towards solutions.

Policies that focus on renewable energy, such as wind or solar power, help reduce the harmful emissions that contribute to climate change. Governments can also create laws that limit pollution, protect forests and wildlife, and ensure that companies follow sustainable practices. Seeing these actions in place helps alleviate the stress of eco-anxiety because it shows that the fight against climate change is not just on our shoulders—it's something being tackled at a higher level as well.

Another way government policy can help is by supporting vulnerable communities that are most affected by climate change. When people see their leaders acting to protect those in need, it creates a sense of fairness and compassion, which is crucial in times of crisis. These policies can include funding for communities affected by natural disasters or supporting farmers struggling with drought. By addressing climate impacts in a just and compassionate way, governments help people feel supported and cared for, which eases anxiety.

Holding Corporations Accountable: What You Can Do

Corporations are some of the biggest contributors to climate change, and they have a huge responsibility to do better. Holding corporations accountable can feel like a big challenge, especially as individuals, but there are ways we can push for change and make our voices heard.

1. Vote with Your Wallet

One of the most powerful ways you can influence corporations is by choosing where you spend your money. Supporting companies that use sustainable practices sends a message that consumers care about the environment. Look for companies that are transparent about their environmental impact, use renewable energy, or make products with minimal packaging. On the other hand, avoiding companies known for harmful practices tells them that they need to change if they want your business. Every purchase you make is like casting a vote for the kind of future you want.

2. Speak Up

Corporations pay attention to their customers. If you're unhappy with a company's environmental practices, let them know. Write a letter, send an email, or use social media to express your concerns. You might feel like one voice doesn't matter, but when many people speak up, it can create pressure for companies to change. Often, companies make changes because they realise their customers expect them to do better.

3. Support Advocacy Campaigns

There are many organisations and campaigns dedicated to holding corporations accountable for their impact on the environment. Supporting these campaigns—whether by signing petitions, donating, or attending events—can help amplify the call for change. These organisations often have more influence and the ability to put direct pressure on corporations, and your support helps them be more effective.

4. Share Information

Knowledge is power, and one of the most effective ways to hold corporations accountable is to share what you know. If you learn about harmful

corporate practices, tell others—whether it's
friends, family, or on social media. Raising
awareness encourages more people to join the
cause, and the more people who demand change,
the more likely companies are to listen.

5. Engage in Boycotts

Sometimes, refusing to buy from a company is the
best way to send a message. When enough people
join a boycott, it can lead to real changes. Boycotts
have successfully pushed companies to change
harmful practices, such as reducing plastic waste or
cutting ties with environmentally damaging
suppliers. If there's a boycott against a company
known for environmental harm, consider
joining—it's a way to show that you care about how
companies impact the planet.

Positive Policy Shifts and Green Innovations

It's easy to focus on the negative aspects of climate change, but there are also many positive changes happening around the world—especially when it comes to policy shifts and innovations that give us hope for the future. Governments and companies are increasingly recognising the need for action, and this is leading to some inspiring developments.

1. Renewable Energy Growth

Governments around the world are investing in renewable energy sources like wind, solar, and hydropower. Countries are setting ambitious targets to reduce their reliance on fossil fuels, and we're seeing rapid growth in clean energy technology. For example, solar power has become one of the fastest-growing energy sources, providing a cleaner, sustainable alternative to coal and oil. These policy shifts towards renewable energy not only help fight climate change but also show us that a sustainable future is possible.

2. Conservation Initiatives

Another positive change is the creation of more protected areas for nature. Governments are setting aside large areas of land and ocean to be conserved, which helps protect wildlife and ecosystems. For example, there have been new policies aimed at creating marine reserves to protect coral reefs and sea life from overfishing and pollution. These conservation initiatives are a sign that the natural world is being valued and protected, which brings hope that we can prevent further loss of biodiversity.

3. Circular Economy Policies

Many countries are beginning to adopt policies that encourage a circular economy—an economy where products are designed to be reused, recycled, or repurposed rather than thrown away. This is a shift from the traditional "take, make, dispose" model, which creates a lot of waste. Policies promoting recycling, reducing single-use plastics, and encouraging companies to make products that last longer are all part of this change. These shifts help reduce the pressure on natural resources and cut down on pollution, which is a major step towards sustainability.

4. Green Innovations

Corporations and innovators are coming up with new technologies and ideas to tackle environmental challenges. For example, electric vehicles are becoming more common, providing a cleaner alternative to gas-powered cars. Innovations in sustainable farming, like vertical gardens and regenerative agriculture, are helping reduce the environmental impact of food production. These innovations are proof that human creativity can be a powerful tool in solving the challenges we face.

5. Policies on Carbon Emissions

Many governments are now implementing stricter rules on carbon emissions, holding companies accountable for their impact on the environment. Cap-and-trade systems, carbon taxes, and incentives for businesses that lower their emissions are all ways that governments are pushing for cleaner practices. Seeing these policies in action can reduce eco-anxiety by showing that progress is being made, and that governments and corporations are being held to account.

Governments and corporations play a significant role in the fight against climate change. When they take action, it makes a big difference—not only for the environment but also for our mental well-being. Policy changes that promote sustainability help reduce eco-anxiety because they show that meaningful action is being taken to address the crisis. Holding corporations accountable can feel daunting, but even small actions—like choosing where to spend your money, speaking up, and supporting advocacy efforts—can create real change.

Positive shifts in policy and green innovations give us hope that a better, more sustainable future is possible. We're all part of this process, and by staying informed, getting involved, and supporting policies and innovations that make a difference, we can help create a world that is healthier and more resilient. Every step forward is a reminder that change is happening, and that gives us hope in the face of uncertainty.

Chapter 10: Coping with Climate Disasters

Preparing Mentally and Physically for Climate-Related Events

Climate disasters—such as hurricanes, floods, wildfires, or heatwaves—can be incredibly frightening. These events remind us of how powerful nature can be, and they often leave us feeling vulnerable. Preparing for these events is an important part of coping with eco-anxiety and reducing the fear that comes with uncertainty. While we can't always predict when a climate disaster will happen, we can take steps to feel more ready, both mentally and physically.

1. Make a Plan

One of the best ways to prepare is to have a plan in place for you and your loved ones. Knowing what to do when a disaster strikes can help you feel more in control. Make sure you have an emergency kit with essentials like water, non-perishable food, medications, flashlights, and important documents. Know the safest routes out of your area if you need to evacuate, and have a list of emergency contacts. Sharing this plan with your family ensures everyone is on the same page and knows what to do, which can bring some peace of mind.

2. Stay Informed

Being informed about the risks in your area and understanding how to respond to different situations can make a huge difference. Know the potential climate risks where you live—whether it's flooding, wildfires, or extreme storms—and stay up-to-date with weather alerts. Having reliable information allows you to act quickly and appropriately, which helps reduce the feeling of helplessness that can come during these events.

3. Prepare Mentally

Preparing mentally is just as important as preparing physically. It's normal to feel anxious when you think about potential climate disasters, but practising mindfulness can help. Taking a few moments each day to meditate, practice deep breathing, or visualize positive outcomes can help you build resilience. This way, when you do face a crisis, you're better able to remain calm and focused.

Remember, being prepared doesn't mean you're expecting the worst—it means you're taking control of what you can, which helps reduce fear and anxiety.

Strategies to Stay Calm in an Emergency

When a climate disaster does happen, it's natural to feel overwhelmed. The fear of the unknown and the urgency of the situation can lead to panic, but having strategies to stay calm can make a big difference in how you respond. Staying calm helps you make better decisions and also provides reassurance to those around you.

1. Focus on Your Breath

In moments of high stress, our breathing often becomes fast and shallow, which can increase feelings of panic. To help calm yourself, try to focus on your breath. Take slow, deep breaths in through your nose and out through your mouth. Counting as you breathe—inhale for four counts, hold for four, exhale for four—can help keep your mind focused and your body relaxed. Deep breathing signals to your brain that it's okay to calm down, even in stressful situations.

2. Break It Down into Steps

In an emergency, the situation can feel overwhelming, but breaking it down into small, manageable steps can help. Instead of focusing on the entire crisis, focus on what you need to do next. For example, if you need to evacuate, focus first on gathering your emergency kit, then on getting everyone safely to the car. Breaking tasks down helps you stay in control and prevents the panic that often comes with trying to take in everything at once.

3. Use a Grounding Technique

Grounding techniques can help bring you back to the present moment when your mind starts racing. One method is the "5-4-3-2-1" technique: identify five things you can see, four things you can touch, three things you can hear, two things you can smell, and one thing you can taste. This exercise helps take your focus off the fear and brings your attention to what's happening right now, helping you stay grounded during a crisis.

4. Lean on Loved Ones

If you're facing a climate disaster with others, don't be afraid to lean on each other for support. Holding someone's hand, sharing a few calming words, or simply staying close can provide a great deal of comfort. Knowing that you're not alone and that you're in this together helps reduce anxiety and keeps everyone focused.

Supporting Others in Times of Crisis

During a climate disaster, supporting others is not only kind, but it can also help reduce your own anxiety. Helping others gives you a sense of purpose, reminds you that you're not powerless, and strengthens bonds that make everyone feel more resilient.

1. Offer Emotional Support

During times of crisis, emotions are high, and it's normal for people to feel scared, overwhelmed, or sad. Offering a listening ear can make a big difference. Sometimes, just being there for someone—letting them talk, cry, or express their fears—can be incredibly comforting. You don't need to have all the answers; your presence alone can provide a great deal of support.

2. Help with Practical Tasks

Helping others with practical tasks during a disaster is another way to provide support. This might mean helping someone pack their belongings, giving them a ride to safety, or sharing supplies. These small acts of kindness not only make a big difference to those in need but also give you something positive to focus on, which can help reduce your own anxiety.

3. Stay Connected

Staying connected during and after a crisis is essential. Check in on neighbours, friends, and family, especially those who may need extra help, such as the elderly or those with young children. Let them know they're not alone and that they have your support. Even a simple phone call can provide a sense of security and comfort, knowing that someone is looking out for them.

4. Be Patient with Others

People react differently to crises—some might be calm, while others might be overwhelmed or even irritable. Being patient and understanding is crucial. Remember that everyone is doing their best to cope, and emotions can be unpredictable. By approaching others with kindness and empathy, you help create a supportive atmosphere that benefits everyone.

5. Take Care of Yourself Too

While supporting others, don't forget to take care of yourself. You can't pour from an empty cup—make sure you're also taking breaks, eating, staying hydrated, and finding moments of calm for yourself. This allows you to be a source of strength for others without burning out.

In all, coping with climate disasters is challenging, but preparing both mentally and physically can help ease the fear that comes with these unpredictable events. By having a plan, staying informed, and knowing what steps to take, you can feel more in control when faced with a crisis. Practising techniques to stay calm—like deep breathing and grounding exercises—can help you navigate emergencies more effectively and provide reassurance to those around you.

Supporting others during these times is not only an act of kindness but also a way to help yourself cope. Whether it's offering a listening ear, helping with practical tasks, or simply staying connected, every bit of support matters and helps strengthen the bonds that keep communities resilient.

Remember, you are not alone. Facing a climate disaster can feel overwhelming, but by preparing, staying calm, and supporting each other, we can get through it together. Every act of preparedness,

every calming breath, and every supportive gesture
brings us closer to a place of safety, strength, and
hope.

Chapter 11: Cultivating Long-Term Hope

The Role of Technology and Innovation in Fighting Climate Change

It's easy to feel discouraged when thinking about climate change, but one of the best sources of hope comes from human creativity—specifically through technology and innovation. Around the world, brilliant minds are working hard to develop new ways to address environmental problems. These technologies are helping us reduce our impact on the planet, making our lives more sustainable, and bringing us closer to a cleaner future.

1. Renewable Energy Innovations

One of the biggest advancements has been in renewable energy. Solar and wind energy have come a long way, becoming more efficient and affordable. Solar panels are now commonly found on rooftops, and large wind turbines dot the countryside, generating clean energy that doesn't harm the planet. Innovations like floating wind farms, solar tiles, and advanced energy storage systems are helping us replace fossil fuels with cleaner alternatives. This shift to renewable energy gives us hope that we can meet our energy needs without damaging the earth.

2. Carbon Capture and Recycling Technologies

Scientists are also developing technologies that can capture carbon dioxide before it enters the atmosphere, or even pull it out of the air. These **carbon capture** innovations help reduce the amount of harmful greenhouse gases in the environment, which is crucial for slowing down climate change. Other innovations, like turning carbon emissions into building materials or fuel, are transforming pollution into useful resources, showing that there are creative solutions even for our toughest challenges.

3. Sustainable Agriculture

Innovations in agriculture are also playing a major role in fighting climate change. Techniques like vertical farming—where crops are grown in stacked layers inside buildings—use less water and space, while producing fresh, healthy food closer to where people live. **Regenerative agriculture** focuses on restoring soil health, which not only helps crops grow better but also absorbs more carbon dioxide. These innovations mean we can feed the world in a way that's sustainable and beneficial for the environment.

4. Electric Vehicles and Green Transport

Transportation is a major source of greenhouse gas emissions, but Electric vehicles (EVs) are offering a cleaner alternative. Cars, buses, and even bicycles powered by electricity are becoming more common, making it easier for people to get around without harming the planet. Charging stations are popping up in cities and on highways, making EVs more practical for everyday use. These advancements are bringing us closer to a future where clean, efficient transportation is the norm.

5. Waste Reduction Technologies

Another area of hope is in waste reduction. New technologies are helping turn plastic waste into reusable materials and making packaging biodegradable, reducing the amount of waste that ends up in landfills or oceans. By using technology to recycle more effectively and produce less waste in the first place, we are moving toward a world that values resources instead of throwing them away.

These technologies remind us that human innovation can be a powerful tool for good. When we look at how far we've come and the incredible solutions being developed, it's easier to feel hopeful about our ability to tackle climate change.

Highlighting Stories of Inspirational Climate Leaders

Sometimes, what we need most is to be reminded of the people who are making a real difference in the fight against climate change. Across the world, there are incredible individuals and groups who are dedicating their lives to protecting the planet. Their stories are a source of hope and inspiration, showing us that one person, or a small group, can have a big impact.

1. Greta Thunberg – The Voice of Youth

Greta Thunberg, a young climate activist from Sweden, began by skipping school on Fridays to protest outside her country's parliament, demanding action on climate change. Her passion and courage quickly caught the world's attention, and she inspired millions of young people across the globe to join her cause. Greta's story is a powerful reminder that anyone, no matter their age, can make their voice heard and create change. Her commitment has encouraged many world leaders to take climate issues more seriously.

2. Wangari Maathai – The Green Belt Movement

Wangari Maathai, an environmental activist from Kenya, founded the Green Belt Movement, which led to the planting of millions of trees across Africa. She understood the connection between the environment, human well-being, and community, and she used tree planting as a way to restore the land, empower women, and bring communities together. Wangari's efforts showed that positive environmental change can also mean social change, improving people's lives while helping the planet.

3. David Attenborough – The Power of Storytelling

David Attenborough, the beloved natural historian, has spent his life bringing the wonders of nature into our homes through his documentaries. By showing the beauty of the natural world and explaining the threats it faces, David has inspired millions of people to care about the environment. His storytelling has helped people understand the urgency of protecting our planet, making a complex issue relatable and real.

4. Indigenous Environmental Protectors

Around the world, Indigenous communities have long been protectors of the environment, living in harmony with the land and advocating for its preservation. People like **Nemonte Nenquimo** of the Waorani people in the Amazon are leading efforts to protect rainforests from deforestation and oil extraction. These communities show us the importance of respecting and preserving nature, as well as the deep wisdom we can learn from those who have lived sustainably for generations.

These leaders—and many more like them—are proof that change is possible, and that dedication and passion can inspire action on a global scale. Their stories remind us that while climate change is a huge challenge, there are people who are making real progress, and we can all play a part.

Creating a Vision for a Sustainable Future

When we think about the future, it's easy to get caught up in worries and fears, especially when we consider the challenges posed by climate change. But cultivating hope means envisioning a future where we've come together to solve these problems—a future that's not just about survival but about thriving in harmony with the natural world.

1. A Future Powered by Clean Energy

Imagine a world where our cities are powered entirely by renewable energy. Solar panels on rooftops, wind farms across the countryside, and energy storage systems that ensure we have power day and night. Clean energy is the backbone of a sustainable future, where we no longer need to rely on fossil fuels that harm the planet. It's a world where our homes, schools, and workplaces are energy-efficient, using technology that makes life more comfortable without damaging the environment.

2. Thriving Ecosystems and Protected Nature

In this future, ecosystems are thriving. Forests have been restored, providing habitats for countless species and absorbing carbon dioxide. Oceans are healthy, teeming with marine life, free from pollution. People visit these natural spaces not just for their beauty but also to reconnect and find peace. Protected areas are respected, ensuring that wildlife has the space to flourish and that future generations can experience the wonder of nature.

3. Sustainable Communities

Sustainable communities are at the heart of this vision. People live in homes that are built with the environment in mind, using materials that are renewable and designed to be efficient. Gardens, both private and community, are everywhere, providing fresh food and green spaces for everyone. Transportation is clean, with electric buses, bikes, and walkable cities making it easy to get around without harming the environment.

4. A Circular Economy

In this future, waste is a thing of the past. Products are made to last, designed to be reused, repaired, or recycled. Companies take responsibility for what they produce, ensuring that nothing ends up polluting the environment. The idea of a circular economy—where everything is part of a cycle, and nothing is wasted—means that we live in a world that respects and preserves resources.

5. A Culture of Care and Community

Perhaps most importantly, this future is one where people care—about each other, about the planet, and about the generations to come. Communities are stronger, people support one another, and there's a shared understanding that our well-being is tied to the health of our environment. Education focuses on sustainability, teaching children to respect and protect the natural world. The culture of care extends from individuals to governments and corporations, all working together to create a better future for everyone.

Cultivating long-term hope means believing in the power of human creativity, the strength of our communities, and the resilience of nature. Technology and innovation are providing us with incredible tools to fight climate change, while inspiring leaders remind us that change is possible, and that our actions matter. Creating a vision for a sustainable future helps us focus on what's possible—on the kind of world we want to build.

This future is not a distant dream—it's something we're working towards every day, with every choice we make, every conversation we have, and every action we take. By imagining this future, we remind ourselves that we have the power to make it real, and that gives us the hope we need to keep going.

Chapter 12: Personal Growth Through Eco-Anxiety

What Eco-Anxiety Can Teach Us About Resilience

Eco-anxiety, while challenging, can also be an opportunity for personal growth. Feeling anxious about climate change is a sign that we care deeply about our planet and our future. It means that we are aware of what's happening around us and that we want to be part of the solution. Learning to manage these emotions can teach us a lot about resilience—the ability to bounce back and stay strong in the face of adversity.

When we feel anxious, it's easy to want to hide from what's causing our fear. But eco-anxiety pushes us to face reality, which can be incredibly difficult but also empowering. By acknowledging our fears, we are practicing courage. Every time we choose to learn more about climate change, take action, or have an open conversation about it, we are building our resilience. We're showing ourselves that, even when things feel overwhelming, we can still move forward.

Eco-anxiety also teaches us about the importance of adaptability. Just as nature adapts to changing conditions, we too must learn to adapt to new challenges. By finding new ways to cope, making lifestyle changes, or joining community efforts, we are adapting to a world that is changing rapidly. This adaptability helps us grow stronger and more capable, not just in dealing with climate change, but in all areas of our lives.

Transforming Anxiety into Empowerment

Anxiety often makes us feel powerless, but it doesn't have to stay that way. One of the most powerful things we can do is to transform our eco-anxiety into something positive—into empowerment. Empowerment means taking back a sense of control, feeling that our actions can make a difference, and finding strength in the face of uncertainty.

1. Take Small, Meaningful Actions

One of the best ways to turn anxiety into empowerment is by taking action, no matter how small. Whether it's reducing plastic use, planting a tree, or switching to renewable energy sources, each action helps create positive change. These small steps remind us that we are not helpless—we are actively contributing to a solution. Each time we make a choice that benefits the environment, we are transforming our anxiety into a force for good.

2. Focus on What You Can Control

A lot of eco-anxiety comes from worrying about things that are beyond our control, like government policies or corporate practices. While it's important to advocate for change, focusing solely on what we can't control can leave us feeling overwhelmed. Instead, focusing on what we can control—like our own choices, how we speak to others, and the actions we take—helps us feel more empowered. Every time we do something positive, no matter how small, we remind ourselves that we have the power to make a difference.

3. Connect with Others

Being part of a community can help transform anxiety into empowerment. When we connect with others who share our concerns, we realise that we are not alone. Working together with like-minded people—whether it's in a local group, an online community, or even just a few friends—makes our efforts more impactful. Together, we can achieve more than we could alone, and this shared effort helps replace feelings of fear with hope and strength.

4. Educate and Advocate

Learning more about climate change and how we can address it can be incredibly empowering. The more we understand, the less intimidating it becomes. Sharing that knowledge with others—whether through conversations, social media, or community events—also helps turn anxiety into action. Educating and advocating remind us that we are part of a larger movement, and our voice matters.

Becoming an Agent of Change in Your Own Life

Eco-anxiety can inspire us to make changes not only for the environment but also in our own lives. By responding to our worries with action, we become agents of change—people who take charge, make a difference, and inspire others to do the same. This journey isn't just about helping the planet; it's also about becoming stronger, more connected, and more fulfilled.

1. Lead by Example.

One of the most powerful ways to become an agent of change is to lead by example. The choices you make every day—how you consume, how you talk about the environment, how you treat others—can inspire those around you. People are often influenced by the actions of others, especially when they see positive changes. By living in a way that reflects your values and care for the planet, you show others that it's possible to make meaningful changes, which can inspire them to do the same.

2. Find Your Passion and Use It for Good.

Everyone has different strengths and interests. Becoming an agent of change means finding what you're passionate about and using that passion to contribute to the cause. Maybe you're a great communicator, and you can use your voice to educate others. Maybe you love gardening, and you can grow food or create a green space for your community. If you're interested in technology, you might explore innovations that support sustainability. Whatever it is, finding your passion makes it easier to stay motivated and turn your concerns into positive contributions.

3. Set Goals and Celebrate Achievements.

Making a difference doesn't always happen overnight, and that's okay. Setting small, achievable goals can help keep you motivated and focused. Whether it's reducing your household waste, switching to renewable energy, or encouraging a friend to join an environmental group, every goal achieved is a step forward. Celebrate these achievements, no matter how small. Each one is a reminder that you are capable of creating change.

4. Inspire Others.

Being an agent of change isn't just about what you do—it's also about inspiring others to act. Share your journey, your challenges, and your successes with friends, family, or your community. When people see the positive steps you're taking, they might feel encouraged to do the same. Your story could be what sparks someone else's journey towards living more sustainably. Remember, change often starts with one person, but it spreads when others are inspired to join in.

In all, eco-anxiety, though challenging, can be a powerful catalyst for personal growth. It teaches us resilience, courage, and the importance of adaptability. By transforming anxiety into empowerment, we can take back control, focus on positive actions, and be part of the solution. Every small action we take, every positive choice we make, and every conversation we have helps transform our fear into something meaningful.

Becoming an agent of change in your own life means leading by example, using your passions to contribute, setting achievable goals, and inspiring others to join you. It's about turning your concern for the planet into actions that make a difference, not just for the environment but also for yourself and your community.

Eco-anxiety is a sign that you care deeply. By using that care as a force for action, you grow stronger, more connected, and more hopeful. Remember, you have the power to make a difference—not just in the world, but in your own life as well. Every step you take, no matter how small, is a step towards a better future, and that is something to be proud of.

Conclusion

Finding Balance Between Awareness and Well-being

Living in a world where climate change is a constant reality means finding a balance between staying informed and taking care of your own well-being. Awareness is important because it helps us understand what is happening and why it matters. But too much focus on the negatives can overwhelm us, leaving us feeling hopeless and anxious. The key is to strike a balance that allows you to stay engaged without sacrificing your mental and emotional health.

It's okay to take breaks. It's okay to disconnect from the news, put your phone down, and spend time doing things that bring you joy. This doesn't mean you don't care—it means you're taking care of yourself so that you can continue to care for the world. Finding that balance helps ensure that your passion for change remains a source of motivation, not exhaustion. Remember, taking care of the planet starts with taking care of yourself.

Holding on to Optimism: Practical Steps for the Future

While the challenges we face are real, it's important to hold on to hope. Optimism is not about ignoring the problems—it's about believing in the possibility of positive change and working towards it. There are practical steps we can take, as individuals and as communities, to build a better future. Each small action adds up, and each effort we make helps create a ripple effect of change.

1. Set Achievable Goals.

One practical way to stay optimistic is to set achievable goals for yourself. These goals could be related to reducing waste, conserving energy, or supporting environmental initiatives. Every time you reach a goal, you're making a positive impact, and that success becomes a reminder that your actions matter. It's easier to stay hopeful when you see the progress you're making, even if it's one step at a time.

2. Connect with Like-Minded People.

Another step is to connect with others who share your values and concerns. When we come together, we feel stronger, more supported, and more capable of facing challenges. Whether it's joining a community group, participating in local events, or simply having conversations with friends and family, these connections help nurture optimism. They remind us that we're not alone, and that many people are working towards the same goal of a better, more sustainable future.

3. Celebrate the Wins

It's important to take time to celebrate the wins, both big and small. Whether it's a local recycling initiative, a global conservation success, or even a change you made in your own life, every win is a step forward. Celebrating these successes helps us stay motivated and reminds us that progress is possible, even when it feels slow.

A Call to Action: From Anxiety to Positive Change

Eco-anxiety is a sign that you care deeply about the world, and that is something to be proud of. It's normal to feel overwhelmed at times, but those feelings don't have to hold you back. Instead, use them as fuel for positive change. You don't need to have all the answers or solve every problem. All you need to do is take one step at a time, and those steps will add up to something meaningful.

1. Start Where You Are.
Begin by making changes in your own life. It could be something as simple as using less plastic, conserving water, or supporting sustainable brands. Each action you take not only helps the planet but also brings a sense of purpose, turning your anxiety into empowerment.

2. Use Your Voice.
Your voice is powerful. Share your thoughts, concerns, and hopes with others. Talk to friends, family, and even your community leaders about why the environment matters to you. By raising awareness and encouraging others to act, you are helping create a culture of change.

3. Be Kind to Yourself.
Lastly, be kind to yourself. This journey is not about perfection—it's about progress. There will be times

when things feel heavy, and it's important to remember that it's okay to take breaks and take care of yourself. You are already making a difference by caring and taking action, no matter how small it may seem.

Embracing hope in an uncertain future is about finding balance, holding on to optimism, and turning anxiety into positive action. We are living in challenging times, but we are not powerless. Every small change we make, every conversation we have, and every step we take moves us closer to a better future.

Together, we can face the challenges of climate change with resilience, compassion, and hope. By caring for ourselves, supporting each other, and taking action, we can turn our eco-anxiety into a powerful force for change. Remember, you are not alone on this journey, and your efforts—no matter how small—make a difference. Let's embrace hope, take action, and create the future we want to see, one step at a time.